Samuel Chester Reid

The History of the Wonderful Battle of the Brig-Of-War General Armstrong

With a British Squadron, at Fayal, 1814

Samuel Chester Reid

The History of the Wonderful Battle of the Brig-Of-War General Armstrong
With a British Squadron, at Fayal, 1814

ISBN/EAN: 9783337081379

Printed in Europe, USA, Canada, Australia, Japan

Cover: Foto ©ninafisch / pixelio.de

More available books at **www.hansebooks.com**

PORTRAIT OF CAPT. SAMUEL CHESTER REID.
From the celebrated painting by Jarvis, 1815.

THE
HISTORY OF THE WONDERFUL BATTLE
OF THE
BRIG-OF-WAR GENERAL ARMSTRONG
WITH A BRITISH SQUADRON,
AT FAYAL, 1814.

THE FAMOUS GUN, LONG TOM.

SKETCH OF THE LIFE OF
CAPTAIN SAMUEL CHESTER REID,
COMMANDER OF THE ARMSTRONG, WHO DESIGNED THE PRESENT FLAG
OF THE UNITED STATES IN 1818. HISTORY OF THE
FLAG. INTERESTING INCIDENTS, ETC.

BOSTON, MASS.:
L. BARTA & CO., PRINTERS.
1893.

Entered according to Act of Congress in the year 1893, by
SAM C. REID,
in the office of the Librarian of Congress at Washington City, D. C.

DEDICATION.

IN gratitude for the patriotic services of that distinguished, brave, and accomplished United States naval officer, COMMODORE RICHARD W. MEADE, in aiding to commemorate the gallant deeds of my father in defence of the honor of his country's flag, the pages of this pamphlet are specially dedicated.

And, generally, to the magnanimous PEOPLE OF THE UNITED STATES OF AMERICA, in appreciation of their noble, generous sentiments in never failing to recognize the heroic valor of their countrymen.

SAM C. REID.

WASHINGTON CITY, D. C., Fourth of July, 1893.

PREFACE.

The design of the publication of this pamphlet is to procure by its sale a fund for the erection, at the National Capital, of a monumental statue of CAPTAIN SAMUEL CHESTER REID, the gallant commander of the private-armed brig-of-war General Armstrong, in commemoration of his heroic valor and distinguished services to his country.

The people of the United States generally will thus be enabled to contribute to this patriotic and praiseworthy object.

This pamphlet gives the historic details of one of the most wonderful and extraordinary naval battles ever fought on the seas, with interesting incidents never before published. It outlines the policy of Great Britain in its efforts to gain from France the possession of the Province of Louisiana and the Mississippi River; the causes which led to the War of 1812; the gigantic scheme of England for the conquest of New Orleans, Louisiana, and Mexico, and the circumstances which led to its defeat; speculations as to the Treaty of Ghent; a sketch of the biography and genealogy of Captain Reid and his services; vindication of our merchant marine; tribute of Senators Voorhees and Evarts; letter of Governor Shelby; history of "Long Tom"; origin and history of the Flag of the United States; historical connection between Admiral Sir Thomas Cochrane and Captain Reid; the song of the General Armstrong; the romance of the celebrated case of the Armstrong; and the poem of James Jeffrey Roche on "The fight of the Armstrong privateer."

LETTER FROM THE SECRETARY OF THE NAVY.

The following extract of a letter from Hon. Hilary A. Herbert, Secretary of the United States Navy, in relation to the sale of this pamphlet, in order to procure a fund for the erection of a monumental statue of Captain Samuel Chester Reid, at Washington City, expresses the approbation of the Navy Department for this project.

NAVY DEPARTMENT.

WASHINGTON, July 15, 1893.

MR. SAM C. REID, Washington, D. C.

DEAR SIR:— . . . I think the purpose you have in view, namely, the raising of money for the purpose of building a monument to your gallant father, is patriotic and noble. . . .

Yours respectfully,

[SIGNED] HILARY A. HERBERT.

EXHIBITS

OF THE

UNITED STATES NAVY DEPARTMENT.

THE following are among the exhibits of the United States Navy Department on board of the MODEL BATTLE SHIP ILLINOIS, and are thus mentioned in the CATALOGUE OF THE EXHIBITS OF THE UNITED STATES NAVY DEPARTMENT, WORLD'S COLUMBIAN EXPOSITION, 1893, as compiled by Lieutenant H. C. Poundstone, United States Navy:

No. 9511. PORTRAIT OF CAPTAIN SAMUEL CHESTER REID.

This officer was born in 1783, and died in 1861; served as acting midshipman in the West India squadron; commanded the private-armed brig General Armstrong, during the War of 1812, and fought one of the most remarkable naval battles on record, at Fayal, one of the Azore Islands, in 1814; he designed the present form of the flag of the United States, as adopted by Congress in 1818. Captain Reid was appointed a sailing master in the United States Navy, which position he held till his death.

No. 9512. THE SWORD OF CAPTAIN SAMUEL CHESTER REID.

This is the battle sabre of Captain Reid which was wielded with such heroic prowess during the engagement with the enemy.

No. 9513. LONG TOM, A FORTY-TWO POUNDER.

One of the guns of the famous private-armed brig-of-war General Armstrong, commanded by Captain Samuel Chester Reid.

The remarkable heroism of Captain Reid and his officers and men is conspicuous in the history of our country. In a conflict with a British squadron, mounting one hundred and thirty-six guns and over two thousand men, this gun did such admirable execution that the British lost over three hundred men and officers, killed and wounded. The Armstrong carried only seven guns and ninety men, and lost but two killed and seven wounded.

The battle took place at Fayal, one of the Azore Islands, on the night of the twenty-sixth and twenty-seventh of September, 1814. The disabling of the squadron, which was a part of the expedition against New Orleans, so delayed Cochrane's fleet at Jamaica that it saved Louisiana from British conquest.

No. 9514. FIGURE-HEAD OF THE PRIVATE-ARMED BRIG GENERAL ARMSTRONG.

This is a quaint and curious looking specimen of the ship carver's art of other days, which has now nearly gone out of existence. Its fantastic coloring is still in a good state of preservation. It was saved by the crew of the Armstrong after she was scuttled on the beach to prevent her falling into the hands of the enemy, and years afterwards was presented to the Naval Institute, at the Boston Navy Yard, by Mr. Dabney, the United States Consul at Fayal.

THE WONDERFUL BATTLE

OF THE

BRIG GENERAL ARMSTRONG

WITH A

British Squadron, at Fayal, 1814.

The wonderful battle between the United States private-armed brig-of-war General Armstrong, and a British squadron, was fought in the waters of Fayal, one of the Azore or Western islands, on the twenty-sixth and twenty-seventh of September, 1814.

The Armstrong was a small brigantine, of only two hundred and forty-six tons, and mounted six long nines with a forty-two pounder, "Long Tom," on a pivot amidships. Her crew consisted of ninety men, including officers. She was commanded by Captain Samuel Chester Reid.

The British squadron was composed of the ship-of-the-line Plantagenet, of seventy-four guns; the frigate Rota, of forty-four guns; and the brig-of-war Carnation, of eighteen guns, with a total force of one hundred and thirty-six guns, and over two thousand men, under the command of Commodore Robert Lloyd. Considering the forces engaged, the Battle of Fayal was the most desperate, bloody, heroic, and romantic naval fight that ever occurred on the seas. That the reader may more fully comprehend the extraordinary results of this remarkable conflict, as affecting the destinies of both England and America at that time, it will be necessary, before describing the battle, to outline what was then England's policy and object in regard to America.

Great Britain had conquered the Canadas from France in 1760, and had for long years endeavored to obtain the possession of the province of Louisiana and the control of the Mississippi River. France, aware of England's designs, made a secret treaty with Spain, in 1763, and turned over the Province to the Spanish authorities, with the agreement that Spain should make a retrocession whenever called for. After a period of nearly four decades, Spain made a recession of Louisiana, in 1801, back to France, and in view of the war with England, Napoleon Bonaparte, on the thirtieth of April, 1803, sold and ceded the province of Louisiana to the United States for the small sum of about fifteen millions, a vast territory now consisting of fifteen States of this Union. On the twentieth of December, 1803, the tri-colored flag was hauled down at New Orleans, and replaced by the Stars and Stripes. Thus were the cherished hopes of England again foiled.

From this period, pending the war between England and France, up to 1808 and 1809, the British navy was "mistress of the seas," having over nine hundred ships of war. Her unscrupulous commanders did not hesitate to commit the most atrocious and flagrant acts by violating the neutrality of any nation to subserve their ends.

In 1804, the British frigate Cambrian, Captain Bradley, entered the harbor of New York, with other cruisers, seized one of our merchant vessels, just arrived, and impressed and carried off a number of her seamen and passengers. In 1806, three British ships of war boarded and burned the French ship Impetueux of seventy-four guns, which had run aground on the coast of North Carolina, a few hundred yards from the shore. Our coasting vessels were frequently fired into, and in some instances some of the crew killed. The notorious Captain Douglas, of the Leopard, subsequently, actually blockaded the port of Norfolk, obstructed our citizens in their ordinary communication between that and other places, and in fact besieged the town on the land side. For all these hostile acts of violence and outrage on our commerce and coast, these insults to our national sovereignty, in violation of the laws of neutrality, England insolently refused to give any satisfaction or make any reparation or apology. Finally, these outrages culminated in 1807, by the infamous attack of his Britannic majesty's ship Leopard on the American frigate Chesapeake, off the capes of Virginia, which, after five years of diplomatic negotiation, determined Congress to declare war against England on the fourth of June, 1812, under the administration of Mr. Madison.

In March, 1814, the allied armies entered Paris. Napoleon had abdicated the throne of France, and was secluded in the isle of Elba. The dove, with its olive branch, had spread its wings over Europe, holding out a lasting peace. The vast fleets of England that had blockaded the European coasts, and the veterans of her armies, were now free to strike a crushing and fatal blow at America's cost and humiliation.

At last the opportunity had arrived for England to achieve her long wished for desire for the conquest of Louisiana. For this purpose, one of the boldest and grandest schemes was devised and planned by England's prime minister, the wily strategist, Lord Castlereagh, in whose hands was then confided the policy of the British Government, the young Prince of Wales reigning at that time as Prince Regent in place of his father, George III., who, being mentally infirm, had been deposed in February, 1811.

A gigantic expedition was arranged by which Negril Bay, in the West Indian island of Jamaica, was made the rendezvous for concentrating the transports and troop-ships of Generals Keane and Packenham, with Wellington's veterans, there to await reinforcements of the immense fleet of

England's navy, under command of Admiral Cochrane, which was to control the Gulf of Mexico. The great scheme was to carry New Orleans by surprise before any defence could be made by any large body of troops, and with the Mississippi River and its coast once in their possession, to seize the country along the Rio Grande, and all west to the Rocky Mountains and the coast of California. "The greatest secrecy was maintained as to the ultimate object of the expedition," says an English writer, in attributing the failure of the expedition to the delay of Commodore Lloyd's squadron, which formed a part of the fleet.

To delude and deceive our Government, and draw its attention away from the contemplated end in view, a demonstration was first made by a part of Cochrane's fleet, which entered the Chesapeake with about sixty sail, and finding no obstacle to impede its progress, proceeded up the Potomac and burned Washington, on the twenty-fourth of August, 1814. A further demonstration was made against Baltimore, all for the purpose of concealing the real design of the expedition for the conquest of Louisiana. Inflated with the pride of his unexpected vandal victory, though at a severe cost, Admiral Sir Thomas Cochrane set sail on the sixth of October, for Jamaica, giving out that his destination was Halifax, while our Government was led to fear an attack on New York.

So sure was England of the triumphant success of this brilliant and magnificent enterprise, that Lord Castlereagh, who was banqueting in Paris at the time the news of the burning of Washington was received, exultingly and openly boasted that it would not be long before Louisiana and the Mississippi River would become the conquered province of Great Britain! But little did England's great prime minister dream, while then sipping his wine, with an extra *goût* of exalted triumph, that his great scheme on the chessboard of war would be checkmated, and the little brig General Armstrong, like an unseen spectre, would dash from his lips the goblet of all his anticipations of the successful conqueror! Nor could it then be foretold that the Battle of Fayal would not only decide the fate of both England and the United States in this war, but the hand of Destiny would save the latter from inconceivable impending calamities, as well as avenge the burning of the capital by a fearful retribution!

During the time when the British General Ross, with his six thousand veteran soldiers from the troop-ships of Cochrane's fleet, was burning and pillaging the American capital, for which he afterwards paid the penalty of his life in his demonstration against Baltimore, the "saucy" little brig General Armstrong was being refitted in the port of New York for her fifth cruise against the enemy. She was a beautiful model, and had been schooner rigged, but Captain Reid, on being induced to take command of her, changed her rig into a brigantine, which made her one of the fastest vessels on the seas. She had a superior armament for boarding or resisting attack, with steel-strapped helmets for the men. She had a picked crew of experienced fighting sailors, all Americans, and among the marines were a number of Kentuckians.

It is but justice to the American sailor here to state that the services and triumphs of our privateers during the war of 1812 have rarely been fully appreciated, and never were ranked or recognized with those of our regular navy. They have been universally ignored in our school histories, and in many so-called histories of the United States. In fact, our private-armed vessels of war, called privateers, and reproachfully classed by some as "freebooters of the seas," were in every respect on a par with the vessels of our regular navy. The only difference was that the one were built, owned, and equipped by our merchants, while the others were built, owned, and equipped by the Government. The officers of the privateers were commissioned by the President, just the same as our naval officers. They were under the same rules and regulations as the regular navy, and subject to the orders and instructions of the Secretary of War (then General John Armstrong, after whom the famous brig was named), there being no Secretary of the Navy at that time. These privateers not only engaged the enemy in many a desperate battle, during the war of 1812, but swept the commerce of England from the ocean.

A distinguished officer of the United States Navy has magnanimously and most truthfully said, "The long delayed, tardy justice to the volunteer or merchant sailor element of this country, which has taken a tremendous part in *all* our maritime wars, should no longer fail to be recognized. For indeed it was the element from which our Revolutionary Navy was *entirely* recruited, and which has since added so much glory to our national prowess."

The Armstrong lay off the Battery, at New York, the admiration of the citizens, awaiting a chance to run the blockade of British war-ships off Sandy Hook. The discipline of her crew was perfect, and her commander, while severely exacting, treated his men with great kindness and consideration, which greatly endeared him to the crew. On the night of the ninth of September, 1814, just two little weeks after the burning of Washington, wind and tide suiting, the Armstrong got under weigh with her great spread of canvas and a ten-knot breeze. At midnight she ran close aboard of an English razee and ship-of-the-line, and as she flew past the "mudscows," as the crew called the clumsy Britishers, she was soon out of range of their guns, and the enemy gave up the chase in the attempted pursuit.

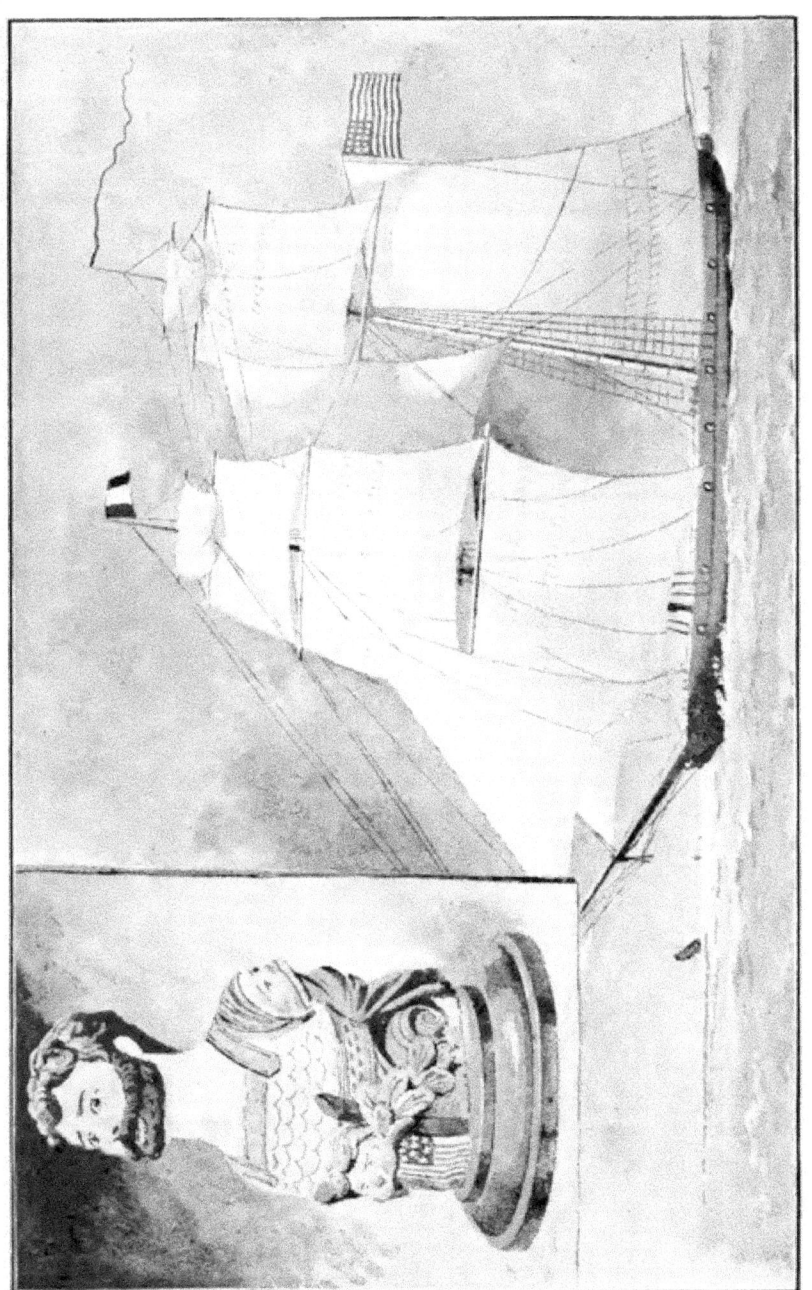

FIGURE-HEAD AND PICTURE OF THE BRIG. GENERAL ARMSTRONG.
From an original painting.

THE BATTLE OF FAYAL.

At noon, on the twenty-sixth day of September, just ten days before Admiral Cochrane sailed from the Chesapeake, the Armstrong made the island of Fayal, and ran into the bay of the town of Da Horta, to refill with water. Fayal is one of the group of the Azore or Western islands, belonging to the kingdom of Portugal, and lies nearly midway between the coast of Portugal and America. The shore of the bay is crescent shaped, and is surrounded by a high sea-wall, in the centre of which lies the castle of Santa Cruz. Opposite, to the eastward, lies the island of Pico, only four miles distant, with its volcanic mountain rising seventy-six hundred feet high. It was in this bay of Da Horta of the island of Fayal, surrounded by the most romantic scenery, that the battle took place. Captain Reid had gone ashore to make arrangements with the American consul, Mr. John B. Dabney, for a supply of fresh water, and had accepted the hospitality of that patriotic gentleman of the old school, to dine with him. In making inquiry about the enemy's cruisers, Captain Reid was informed by Mr. Dabney that none had visited those islands for several weeks. About 5 P. M. Captain Reid returned aboard his vessel with the consul and several gentlemen in company. While they were conversing, it being nearly sundown, the British brig-of-war Carnation suddenly hove in sight close under the northeast headland of the harbor, and entering the bay anchored within half a cable's length of the Armstrong. Soon after the frigate Rosa and ship-of-the-line Plantagenet followed, and came to anchor in the roads, the squadron being on its way to join Cochrane's fleet at Jamaica.

Commodore Lloyd, who commanded the squadron, had previously been informed by the pilot out at sea that the Armstrong was in the harbor, and he at once determined upon her capture. The brig Carnation immediately began signalizing with the fleet, threw out four large launches or boats, and commenced passing arms into them. All these movements could be seen, and the orders given were distinctly heard on board the Armstrong. At the same time the British brig made every preparation to intercept the privateer should she attempt to escape. Although Captain Reid had been assured of the perfect safety of his vessel by the American consul, being in a neutral port, he now felt certain, from the manœuvres of the fleet and the preparations going on, that there would be trouble, and he accordingly told the gentlemen that they had better go on shore. After their departure a council was held among the officers of the Armstrong, and it was first suggested that they should make an effort to get out to sea; but the wind being very light, it was determined to haul close in under the guns of the castle for protection.

Captain Reid immediately gave secret orders to clear the deck for action, and cautioned the crew to make as little noise as possible. He then cut his cable, got out sweeps and commenced pulling in shore to the castle. The Carnation immediately dropped her topsails and made sail, to prevent the privateer from going out of the harbor should she attempt it, while the boats, which were lying alongside, were ordered in chase of the Armstrong. It was now about eight o'clock in the evening. The moon, which was near its full, was gradually rising, and silver-sprinkling with its beams the beautiful bay, the hills of Da Horta, and Mount Pico, while not a ripple broke the stillness of the glittering surface, save the splash of the oars of the four large launches, well armed, carrying about forty men each, which were pulling swiftly towards the privateer. Captain Reid immediately ceased pulling towards the shore, let go an anchor, and got springs on his cable so as to bring the vessel broadside to the enemy.

At this time one of the large launches, which was considerably in the advance, pulled up under the stern of the Armstrong, when Captain Reid, with speaking-trumpet in hand, being in his shirt-sleeves, and all hands at quarters, hailed the boat three times. No answer was returned except by one of the sailors, who asked in a gruff voice what was the matter. The officer replied: "Make no answer, sir; pull away, my lads," and the next moment the word was given to "toss oars," and with their boat-hooks they hauled alongside under the port quarter of the privateer. The officer in the boat then cried out: "Fire and board, my lads," and as the men rose from their seats, Captain Reid instantly gave the word to his marines to fire, which was almost simultaneous on the part of both. One man on board the privateer was instantly killed, and the first lieutenant, Fred. A. Worth, a brother of the late General Worth, of the United States Army, was wounded. The men in the boat were severely cut up, and they cried out for quarter, while the other three boats, pulling up at full speed on the starboard side, immediately opened their fire. They were received with a full broadside of grape and canister, which was followed by the shrieks and groans of the wounded and dying. A fierce struggle now ensued, in which the enemy made a desperate attempt to board; but staggered and appalled by the galling fire of the privateer, they cried out for quarter, and the boats pulled off in a sinking condition with great loss, Captain Reid refusing to take them prisoners.

The General Armstrong then weighed anchor and pulled in toward the shore, about half-pistol shot from the castle, where she was moored head and stern near the beach, with her port side next to the shore. The Carnation, in the meanwhile, sailed down to the fleet, and it was soon evident that they had determined on a more formidable attack. The American consul at this time had written a note to the Portuguese Governor, demanding protection for the privateer, but the Governor simply despatched a note to Admiral Lloyd, requesting him to abstain from further hostilities. To this note Lloyd replied that, as the Americans had first fired into one of their boats without any provocation, he now determined to take the privateer at all hazards, and, if protection were afforded her, he would fire into the town.

About 9 P. M., the wind having breezed up, the enemy's brig was observed standing in with a large fleet of boats in tow, numbering fourteen, and carrying between forty and fifty men each, armed with carronades, swivels, blunderbusses and musketry, making an aggregate force of at least five hundred and sixty men. When within gunshot, the boats cast off from the brig, and took their stations in three divisions under cover of a small reef or island of rocks, within musket-shot of the privateer. The brig kept under way to act with the boats in case the privateer attempted to escape. In the meantime terror and consternation had spread through the town. The windows of the houses nearest the scene were filled with women, and the sea-walls were crowded with the inhabitants, awaiting with intense excitement and breathless expectation the coming attack. There lay the American brig with her tall, tapering spars, sleeping on the moonlit waters as quiet and as peaceful as an over-wearied child. There she lay, like the apparition of a phantom ship; not a movement was to be seen, not a sound was heard to break the stillness of her decks, and seemingly deserted, from the death-like silence which prevailed. Notwithstanding, Captain Reid had made every preparation to receive the enemy on all sides, and his crew were then lying concealed at their quarters. In this position the belligerents remained for nearly three hours, watching each other with painful interest. When it is considered that the crew of the Armstrong had nothing to gain, and had no motive for remaining by their vessel but the defence of their country's honor, when they

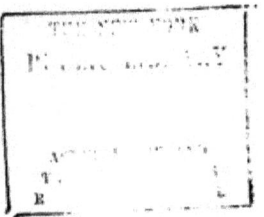

MOONLIGHT BATTLE BETWEEN THE GENERAL ARMSTRONG AND THE BRITISH SQUADRON.
From a painting by Von Beest, 1850.

saw the terrible odds that opposed them, and which threatened a fearful retribution, with no hope of reward except death for the defence of the American flag, while a leap to the shore held out to them the inducement of safety, it is remarkable that they stood so firm, and their wonderful discipline and courage may be imagined.

At length, at midnight, the enemy seemed resolved upon the attack, and the boats were observed in motion. Instead of approaching by divisions, as Captain Reid expected, they came on in solid column in a direct line. When about twenty-five yards off, Captain Reid ordered his men to stand by after the fire, to run in the guns and lash in the ports, in order to prevent the enemy from getting through the portholes on boarding, as they would not have time to reload the guns before the enemy would be alongside. The men were then cautioned to wait for the word, and to be sure of their object. The Long Tom, a heavy forty-two pounder, placed on a pivot amidships, was sighted with fearful accuracy. On came the British boats with undaunted intrepidity, when they were again hailed by Captain Reid, but no answer was returned. The fatal command was then given, and a tremendous fire was opened on the enemy, the thunder and crash of which broke the charmed stillness of the before quiet midnight scene. The discharge of our Long Tom rather staggered them. Reeling back and recoiling from the missiles of death, they warmly returned the fire, remanned their oars and giving three cheers, came on most spiritedly. The crew of the privateer asked if they should return the cheer? "No," replied Captain Reid, "no cheering until we have gained a victory." In a moment they succeeded in gaining the bow and starboard quarter of the Armstrong. The cry of the officers commanding the boats was, "Up and board, my lads — no quarter!" At the same instant they opened a terrific fire with carronades, swivels, blunderbusses and musketry. They were gallantly met by the crew of the privateer in their black leather boarding caps, strapped with steel, looking like demons, with boarding-pikes, muskets, battle-axes, pistols and cutlasses. The vessel soon became one broad sheet of fire, the red glare of which strangely contrasted with the brilliant light of the moon, now riding high in mid-heaven. Shrieks and yells, orders and oaths, amid the clang of sabres, were heard on both sides through the din and roar of the musketry. Again and again the enemy, led by their officers, attempted to gain the decks of the privateer, but were repulsed at all times with immense loss. The battle now raged with the greatest fury. The Americans fought with the desperation of fiends. Making a last desperate effort to board, the enemy gained the spritsail-yard and bowsprit of the Armstrong, and were pressing their way to her decks, when the American sailors, wielding their battle-axes, sabres, and pikes with the skill and might of knights of old, drove back England's best and bravest men with horrid slaughter. The second lieutenant of the Armstrong, Mr. Alex. O. Williams, was killed at this moment while gallantly leading on his forward division; and the third lieutenant, Mr. Robert Johnson, also fell dangerously wounded. At the same instant Captain Reid, who commanded the after division, was engaged beating off two large launches, the men and officers of which had succeeded in climbing up the sides of the privateer. One of the latter, the first lieutenant of the Rota, William Matterface, who commanded the attack, had engaged Captain Reid in a hand-to-hand fight with cutlasses, and once or twice came near overpowering him. Captain Reid, being left-handed, used his right in firing pistols, which the powder boys handed him, while he continued to fight with the British lieutenant with his left hand, disdaining to shoot down his brave adversary. At last the British lieutenant, making a feint, brought down a desperate blow, which Captain Reid had just time to break the force of, cutting the captain slightly across the head and nearly severing his thumb and forefinger. Before the Englishmen could recover, Captain Reid struck him down and he fell back a corpse into the boat.

It was at this critical juncture that Captain Reid was informed of the death of his second lieutenant, and that his third lieutenant was badly wounded. Having succeeded in beating the boats off the quarter, and thus left the only officer on the deck, he perceived that the fire had slackened on the forecastle. At once rallying the whole of the after division, they rushed forward with a shout and opened a fresh fire, while he ordered the forward division to heave cold shot into the boats and sink them, as those men were out of cartridges. The enemy, appalled with consternation and dismay, fell back to their boats and retreated, when Captain Reid bringing the Long Tom to bear upon them, fired the gun himself (which flew off the carriage), doing fearful destruction, and ending in the total defeat of the British. Then it was that Captain Reid cried out, "Now is the time to cheer, my boys," and three wild, enthusiastic cheers re-echoed over the bay from shore to shore. The Americans among the crowd on the sea-walls hailed the Armstrong, and asked if Captain Reid was safe, and, being answered in the affirmative, gave three tremendous cheers in return.

The scene which now presented itself was one of indescribable horror. The silvered waters of the bay were crimsoned with blood. Dark forms of numerous dead bodies floated around on every side, while the groans and death shrieks of the wounded struggling around the boats pierced the very air. Many of the boats had been sunk. Two large launches belonging to the frigate Rota lay alongside the privateer, with two other boats, literally loaded with their own dead. In a boat belonging to the Plantagenet all were killed save four. In another boat which had contained fifty souls, but one solitary officer escaped, and he was wounded. Four boats floated ashore full of dead bodies. Some of the boats were left with but a single man, while others had but three or four to row them. The termination was nearly a total massacre. This action lasted about forty minutes. The English force, estimating forty men to a boat, was about five hundred and sixty men. The English themselves acknowledged a loss in this attack of one hundred and twenty killed and one hundred and thirty wounded, but it must have been far greater.

The deck of the Armstrong, which was in great confusion, and slippery with human gore, was now cleared up, the Long Tom re-mounted, and preparations made for a fresh action, should the enemy again attack her. About this time Captain Reid received the following note from the American consul: —

CAPTAIN REID,

Dear Sir: — You have performed a most brilliant action in beating off fourteen boats of the British ships in this road. They say they will carry the brig, cost what it will, and that the English brig will haul close in to attack you at the same time the boats do. My dear fellow, do not uselessly expose yourself, if again attacked by an overwhelming force, but scuttle the brig near the beach and come on shore with your brave crew.

      Yours truly,
          J. B. DABNEY.

Two o'clock Tuesday morning, Sept. 27, 1814.

This note was brought on board the Armstrong by Charles W. Dabney, a son of the consul, then twenty years of age, who afterwards succeeded his father.

Captain Reid then went on shore, and after receiving the congratulations of the consul, was informed that the Governor had again written to Commodore Lloyd, remonstrating against any further attack, but Lloyd sent for answer that he was determined on the capture of the privateer, and that if the Governor suffered the Americans to injure her in any manner he should consider the place an enemy's port and treat it accordingly. Returning on board, Captain Reid gave up all hope of saving his vessel, but determined to defend her to the last. He accordingly ordered the dead and wounded to be taken on shore, and prepared for the worst.

At daylight on the morning of the twenty-seventh, the Carnation was observed under weigh, and stood close in for the privateer, when she immediately opened a heavy fire with all her force. The crew of the Armstrong, as if supernatural spirits, or holding charmed lives, still grimly stood by their little bark, returning broadside for broadside with wonderful effect, Long Tom doing splendid execution. The maintopmast of the Carnation soon fell by the board, and she became so much cut up in her hull and rigging, and with the loss of men, that her guns became silenced and she was forced to retire. It was a sublime spectacle, that of the little privateer, with but a handful of men, fighting a hopeless battle against such tremendous odds, in vindication of her rights and her country's honor, with her colors flying in reckless defiance.

Finding all further resistance fruitless, Captain Reid scuttled his vessel to prevent her capture, and then, with his gallant crew, took to their boats and went on shore. The Carnation, soon after, perceiving that the Armstrong was deserted, sent two armed boats to seize her, but finding she was scuttled, they set her on fire, when she blew up in a blaze of glory, and thus ended the fate of this famous little craft.

In the three engagements that occurred with the Armstrong, according to a fair estimate of the whole number engaged, of the British squadron, their loss was two hundred and ten killed, and one hundred and forty wounded, making a total of three hundred and fifty, of which it will be seen a majority were killed. The loss of the Armstrong, marvellous to state, was but two killed, and seven wounded!

After the burning of the Armstrong, Commodore Lloyd, frenzied with disappointment and athirst for revenge, demanded that the Governor should deliver up her crew as prisoners of war. The Governor refused, on the ground that it would be in violation of his neutrality, when Lloyd threatened to send five hundred men on shore to take them, dead or alive. Thus threatened, Captain Reid and his men, with their arms, took refuge in an old deserted Gothic convent, knocked away the draw-bridge, ran up the American flag, and bid defiance to the foe, saying, " No surrender until captured." The British commodore quailed under this last demonstration of American courage, and feared to execute his threat.

The final act of this naval tragical drama was the very essence and height of patriotic valor and heroism. The splendid courage and personal prowess by which Captain Reid, his officers and crew, had achieved a glorious victory over the immensely superior force of the British squadron, was never exceeded by the exploits in the olden days of romantic chivalry, as narrated by Washington Irving in his " Conquest of Granada." Yet all this time he was ignorant that he had performed one of the grandest feats of modern or ancient warfare on the seas; that by his undaunted courage in defeating and disabling the British squadron he had saved Louisiana from England's conquest. He was only conscious that he had done his duty in vindicating the honor of his country, and defending untarnished the sovereignty of the American flag. This alone induced him and his noble crew to peril their lives against such fearful odds, and to perform such prodigies of valor!

That no charge of national prejudice and exaggeration of this wonderful conflict may be made, we give the following vivid account by an English gentleman, who was an eye-witness of the scene, in a letter to William Cobbett, Esq., at London, dated Fayal, fifteenth of October, 1814, and published in *Cobbett's Weekly Register*, Dec. 10, 1814. The writer in giving the number of British killed at over one hundred and twenty, and the wounded at ninety in the midnight attack, does not include the loss in the first and last engagement. After mentioning the arrival of the Armstrong and the squadron, he says:

"The authorities all considered the American privateer perfectly secure, and that His Majesty's officers were too well acquainted with the respect due to a neutral port to molest her; but, to the great surprise of everyone, about nine in the evening four boats were despatched, armed and manned, from His Majesty's ships, for the purpose of cutting her out. It being about full moon, the night perfectly clear and calm, we could see every movement made. The boats approached with rapidity toward her, when, it appears the captain of the privateer hailed them, and told them to keep off, several times. They, notwithstanding, pushed on, and were in the act of boarding before any defence was made by the privateer. A warm contest ensued on both sides. The boats were finally repulsed with great loss.

"After the first attack all the inhabitants were gathered about the walls, expecting a renewal of the fight. The American, now calculating on a very superior force being sent, cut his cables, and rowed the privateer within half cable's length of the fort, where he moored her, head and stern. At midnight fourteen launches were discovered to be coming in rotation for the purpose. When they got within gunshot a tremendous and effectual discharge was made from the privateer, which threw the boats into confusion. They now returned a spirited fire, but the privateer kept up so continual a discharge it was almost impossible for the boats to make any progress. They finally succeeded, after immense loss, to get alongside of her, and attempted to board at every quarter, cheered by the officers with a shout of 'No quarter,' which we could distinctly hear, as well as their shrieks and cries. The termination was near about a total massacre. Three of the boats were sunk, and but one poor solitary officer escaped death in a boat that contained fifty souls. He was wounded. The Americans fought with great firmness. Some of the boats were left without a single man to row them; others with three and four. The most that any one returned with was about ten. Several boats floated ashore full of dead bodies.

"With great reluctance I state that they were manned with picked men, and commanded by the first, second, third, and fourth lieutenants of the Plantagenet; first, second, third, and fourth ditto of the frigate, and the first officer of the brig; together with a great number of midshipmen. Our whole force exceeded four hundred men. But three officers escaped, two of whom are wounded. This bloody and unfortunate contest lasted about forty minutes. Nothing more was attempted until daylight next morning, when the Carnation hauled in alongside and engaged her. The privateer still continued to make a most gallant defence. These veterans reminded me of Lawrence's dying words, of the Chesapeake, 'Don't give up the ship.' The Carnation lost one of her topmasts and her yards were shot away. She was much cut up in her rigging and received several shots in her hull. This obliged her to haul off to repair, and to cease firing.

"The Americans now finding their principal gun, Long Tom, and several others dismounted, deemed it folly to think of saving her against so superior a force. They therefore scuttled her and went ashore. Two boats' crews were soon after despatched from our vessels, which went on board, took out some provisions, and set her on fire. For three days after we were employed in burying the dead that washed on shore in the surf. The number of British killed exceeds one hundred and twenty, and ninety wounded. After burning the privateer, Commodore Lloyd made a demand on the Governor to deliver up the Americans as his prisoners, which the Governor refused. He threatened to send five hundred men on shore and take them by force. The Americans immediately retired, with their arms, to an old Gothic convent, knocked away the adjoining draw-bridge, and determined to defend themselves to the last. The Commodore, however, thought better than to send his men. . . . The squadron was detained ten days at Fayal repairing damages and in burying their dead. Two sloops-of-war, the Thais and Calypso, which arrived two days afterwards, were sent back to England with their wounded.

"Being an eye-witness to this transaction, I have given you a correct statement as it occurred.

With respect, I am, etc.,

H. K. F."

THE FIGURE-HEAD OF THE ARMSTRONG.

At the time the Armstrong was scuttled, and the crew were deserting their gallant craft, some of the sailors cried out, "We must save the 'Old General,' lads," as they called the figure-head, for which it seems they had a great affection. No sooner said, than with their battle-axes they severed from the bow the grim-looking bust of the "Old General," which had been a silent witness of their victory, and bore it in triumph to the shore.

This quaint specimen of the ship-carver's art of the days bygone, which once ranked equal to the sculptor's, was placed over the gates leading to the grand mansion of the American consul. For years it was decorated every Fourth of July by the Dabneys, with flowers and the American flag. It was called by the Portuguese peasantry "El Santo Americano," the American Saint, who never failed to cross themselves as they passed by it.

In later years, the American consul, Mr. Charles B. Dabney, son of John B. Dabney, presented this venerable relic to the Naval Lyceum, at Boston, Mass., where it now remains in a good state of preservation.

INTERESTING INCIDENTS.

INTERVIEW OF BRITISH OFFICERS WITH CAPTAIN REID.

After it became evident that Commodore Lloyd did not intend to execute his threat to take Captain Reid and his crew prisoners, they left their quarters in the old convent and returned to the town of Horta.

Several British officers, who had come ashore to attend the burial of their deceased comrades, sent a note to Captain Reid, who was then staying at the house of Consul Dabney, with the request that he would meet them at the British consul's.

Mr. Dabney, who was of the opinion that it was only a ruse to arrest Captain Reid or bring about a duel, counselled him not to go. But Reid said he did not apprehend any indignity, and not to go would be treating them with discourtesy. He accordingly dressed in full uniform, with sash and sabre, and as he approached the quarters of the British consul he observed a number of British officers standing in front of the house, who recognizing him, lifted their caps and gave him a cheer, to the great surprise of Captain Reid.

On being invited to enter the house, and after the compliments of the day were passed, one of the lieutenants said, "We have desired the pleasure of your company, Captain, in order to settle a question among ourselves, as to whether or not you and your crew wore steel shirts of mail during the battle? For both our men and officers are confident that they saw our bullets strike your crew and yourself frequently, and they glanced off like hail!"

Captain Reid laughed at this charge, and replied, "Why, gentlemen, I can assure you that the only steel armor that my officers and men wore was their cutlasses and steel-strapped helmets. As for myself, I admit that your bullets tickled my ears so often that I was almost afraid to turn my head. But you saw I was in my shirt sleeves, and I pledge you, on the honor of a sailor, that the only shirt of mail I wore was a *linen shirt*, which I don't deny was a *shirt of a male!*" A hearty laugh followed, which ended in several bottles of wine being opened and a jolly time.

This reception by the British officers of their deadly foe was certainly remarkable under the circumstances, and proved that by the laws of hospitality British honor was inviolable.

GENERAL JACKSON'S OPINION.

This remarkable battle was the last fought upon the seas in the war with England, while that of New Orleans was the last fought upon the land; though so widely apart, the chain of destiny has linked them close together. When General Jackson afterwards learned that a portion of the fleet which was engaged in the assault upon New Orleans was composed of the same vessels which attacked the Armstrong, he expressed the opinion that but for the determined bravery of

Captain Reid in resisting the enemy, he (Jackson) would never have fought the battle of New Orleans, but that, most probably, the battle ground would have been nearer the shores of his own State.

RETRIBUTION.

A most singular case of retribution connected with the burning of Washington City and the battle of New Orleans was related by the late Commodore Ap Catesby Jones. It seems that Lieutenant G. Pratt, of her Britannic Majesty's frigate Seahorse, led a storming party of marines at Washington, and in looking up at the monument erected to our naval officers at Tripoli, then at the west front of the Capitol, which represented the Muse of History recording with a pen the brave deeds of our fallen heroes, Pratt with his sword broke the hand and took out the pen as a trophy, saying, "The Muse of History needed no pen to record the deeds of runaway cowards!" Afterwards, Catesby Jones, then a lieutenant in command of our gunboats on Lake Pontchartrain during the attack on New Orleans, came in conflict with some British boats commanded by Lieutenant Pratt, whom Jones killed in the conflict with his own sword, but was overpowered, however, and taken prisoner. On being removed to the ship of Lieutenant Pratt, the British officers showed Jones the identical marble pen which Pratt had kept as a trophy. This statue is now at the Naval Academy, Annapolis, Md.

A CONTRAST.

To show the unparalleled victory of the battle of the Armstrong it is stated that in the great naval engagement off Cape Vincent in 1797, between a Spanish fleet of twenty-seven ships-of-the-line and twelve frigates, and a British squadron of fifteen ships-of-the-line and seven frigates and two sloops-of-war, the British acknowledged a loss of seventy-three killed and two hundred and twenty-three wounded, making a total of two hundred and ninety-six. Yet in this tremendous conflict, which lasted over six hours, the English did not lose as many men as they did in trying to capture a little brig of only seven guns! Admiral Jervis, who commanded the British fleet, having defeated the Spaniards, was created an earl by the king of England, and granted a pension of twenty-five thousand dollars a year; while Captain Reid and his men were granted the privilege of prosecuting their claim for their losses before Congress for over half a century, and died without receiving one cent of recompense, thus proving the ingratitude of republics.

The news of the Battle of Fayal reached the United States about the middle of November, 1814; the reverses which had attended our arms on land, the bankrupt condition of the Government, and the burning of our national capital, had thrown a general gloom and despondency over the country. Under these circumstances, the news of the battle of the Armstrong and the extraordinary victory sent a thrill of joy and enthusiasm through the hearts of the American people. But our Government was as ignorant as Captain Reid at the time, that the gallant defence of the little brig Armstrong was to be the means of saving Louisiana from becoming another empire of India, by the grasp of England, and winning for General Jackson the highest pinnacle of fame, glory, and civic honors, by the success of his great victory at New Orleans.

All was ready at Jamaica. The troopships and transports with twelve thousand veterans, under Generals Packenham and Keene, were eager for the fray. Admiral Sir Thomas Cochrane, as he paced the deck of his flagship, was impatiently awaiting the arrival of Lloyd's squadron. How could he know that, when his fleet was sailing past the Capes of the Chesapeake, on the sixth of October, Lloyd was at that very time at Fayal burying his dead and repairing damages, causing the delay of his squadron for ten or twelve days? Finally, when Lloyd's squadron arrived in Negril Bay in its crippled condition, he was loaded with bitter reproaches by Cochrane, Packenham, and Keene, and a further detention of a week followed.

At this time, General Jackson's headquarters were at Mobile. On the seventh of November he had driven the British forces from the neutral Spanish town of Pensacola, and on his return to Mobile had learned of the suspected designs of the British fleet against New Orleans. By a forced march of his two thousand Tennessee militia, he arrived at New Orleans on the second day of December. Cochrane's fleet arrived at Lake Borgne on the sixth of December, just *four days* afterwards. New Orleans was then utterly defenceless. It is evident that if Cochrane's fleet had arrived fifteen days sooner, the period of its delay, say the twentieth of November, the British troops could have taken possession of New Orleans before any possible defence could have been made. And even as it was, General Jackson had barely time to check the enemy by the affair of the twenty-third of December.

On the occasion of a resolution in the United States Senate, in 1890, to strike a gold medal in commemoration of the services of Captain Reid, whose battle sabre was offered by his son as a free gift to the United States, the Honorable Senator Daniel W. Voorhees, in a speech of thrilling eloquence, said :

"But for the terrific injury inflicted on Lloyd's forces at Fayal, the British would have reached New Orleans as soon, if not much sooner than General Jackson. Had this happened that city would have fallen without a blow. . . .

"It is my simple task on this occasion to show that the sword now offered for the acceptance of the Government so guarded the passage-ways of the ocean and so crippled and retarded the enemy, that time was gained by which General Jackson prepared for and won the immortal victory at New Orleans. No such battle would have been fought, no such victory won, but for the stubborn and invincible courage of Captain Reid and his crew at Fayal."

The Hon. William M. Evarts, Senator from New York, followed in this glowing tribute to Captain Reid :

"Mr. President, I have no need to add anything to the eloquent homage paid to the great fame of Captain Reid. Every word that the Senator from Indiana [Mr. Voorhees] has said is as truthful as it was eloquent. . . . The sword is offered us and the matter brought thus to our attention, and we, with shame and remorse, if I do not use too strong words, feel that it has been a shame and disgrace to the people of this country that a medal has never been struck in honor of an event so glorious to the prowess not only of our great captain in this battle, but honorable to human nature.

"There is not to be found in the classics or in modern history any stronger instance of personal prowess performed in modern times, that used to be done under the old warfare of personal prowess. But for Captain Reid that fight would not have been made ; and but for Captain Reid that battle would not have been won. So strong is this simile under the most diverse circumstances, that it may be said of Captain Reid as was said of Horatius at the bridge : 'If he had not kept the bridge, who would have saved the town?' And Rome was 'the town,' and 'the bridge' was across the Tiber. This battle in the port of Fayal was the bridge that he kept that saved the town of New Orleans, and saved the honor of the country."

The Honorable Senator from Ohio [Mr. John Sherman] antagonized this resolution, and by his opposition it went over, and was never acted upon.

LETTER OF GOVERNOR SHELBY.

The following letter from that distinguished veteran warrior and statesman, Governor Isaac Shelby, of Kentucky, to Captain Reid, illustrates the enthusiasm which prevailed throughout the West, on the news being received of the battle of the Armstrong:

"Frankfort, Ky., May 8, 1815.

Sir: — The return of peace to our country upon honorable terms, with a national character exalted in an eminent degree, affords us leisure to review the various conflicts in which that character has been developed.

"On the ocean, where we had most to dread, we have found a rich harvest of glory; and the American tars have secured to themselves the admiration of the world. To the officers and crews of our public vessels much is due, and the nation, through its public functionaries and in other forms, has fully demonstrated its gratitude. We are not less indebted to the officers and crews of our private armed vessels. Instances of talent, skill, discipline, and of a determined, unconquerable bravery have been manifested by our privateersmen. When their situations might have presented to ordinary minds sufficient inducement for avoiding the contest, nothing but a generous and noble patriotism could have led to such deeds. I have no reason to believe that the nation at large is not fully impressed with the gratitude due to this class of our heroes. But I have regretted that there have been so few demonstrations of that sentiment; you will, therefore, although a stranger to you, permit me, for myself individually and on behalf of the State over which I have the honor to preside, to assure you that the conduct of yourself and of your officers and crew in defence of the General Armstrong in the port of Fayal merits the first applause of the nation, and is duly appreciated by our citizens.

"No one conflict during the war has placed the American character in so proud a view.

"The baseness of the attack in a neutral port, the overwhelming force of the assailants, the small prospect of success to yourself and crew, and the unparalleled disparity of loss, demonstrated a combination of talents, skill, and heroism seldom equalled and never surpassed. I trust our Government will fully appreciate your services.

"May you, your officers and crew, long live to enjoy the laurels you so nobly won.

"I have the honor to be, with high consideration of respect and esteem, your most obedient, humble servant,

ISAAC SHELBY.

Captain Samuel C. Reid, late Commander of the United States Privateer General Armstrong."

These exalted and noble sentiments will be the more appreciated when it is recalled that Governor Shelby, as an officer of the Revolutionary War, greatly distinguished himself at the battle of King's Mountain, in October, 1780, and afterwards led his brave Kentuckians, in 1813, against his old enemy in the campaign of the Northwest, with General Harrison. He was born in Maryland, in 1750, and twice served as Governor of Kentucky.

INCIDENTS OF THE TREATY OF GHENT.

In connection with the failure of Lord Castlereagh's great expedition, and the circumstances which led to it, it will be interesting to note that the British Government, during the year 1813, had shown a disposition for a reconciliation and for peace. The Prince Regent was in favor of a cessation of hostilities. But the wily Castlereagh had over-ruled him in order to carry out his great scheme of conquest. Russia had previously offered to act as mediator, but the offer was rejected by the British Ministry.

Finally, early in January, 1814, Commissioners were appointed by the two powers to negotiate a treaty of peace. The Ministry kept the American Commissioners waiting month after month by putting them off on dilatory pleas, first proposing one place and then another for the negotiations. In this way, after six months' delay, the Commissioners of the two governments met at Ghent, in Belgium, in August, 1814, at which time Cochrane's fleet was sailing up the Potomac for the attack on Washington!

Every resort was made to procrastinate and protract the sessions of the Commission in order to gain time, which is shown by the fact that the treaty was not finally concluded until the twenty-fourth of December, 1814, the night previous to which General Jackson had driven back General Keene's troops who were marching on New Orleans, and as we have seen, Castlereagh was expecting that it had already fallen!

About the twenty-fifth of October, after the rejoicing by the British Ministry over the news of the burning of Washington had hardly subsided, the British sloops-of-war Thais and Calypso had arrived, loaded with their wounded from the battle between the Armstrong and Lloyd's squadron, and the details of their dead buried at Fayal. A gloom of sorrow spread over England and filled the land with grief.

Whether this news had any effect on the British Commission, or daunted the hopes of Lord Castlereagh, can easily be conjectured. As to the question, whether the English Government would have stood by the treaty in good faith or not, in case of the conquest of Louisiana, it is a matter of broad speculation. The precedents of the faithlessness and treachery of England in violating treaties and the laws of nations were numerous, and there was but little confidence to be put in her diplomatic negotiations. It is most remarkable that the subject of the right of search and impressment of our seamen, the chief cause of the war, were passed over in the Treaty of Ghent without any stipulation whatever, especially as the treaty with England, made in 1806, was ignored and rejected by President Jefferson, because the right of search and impressment were not fully disavowed, and he became so indignant that he refused to submit it to the Senate.

Mr. Clay, one of the Commissioners of the treaty of Ghent, had but little faith in the honor of the British Government, knowing that its treaty obligations were never respected whenever conflicting with its interest and policy. He is said to have expressed the belief that, if General Jackson had been defeated at New Orleans, with the Mississippi River in possession of the British fleet, England would no more have hesitated to nullify the Treaty of Ghent than she did the Treaty of Amiens with Bonaparte, which obligated her to withdraw her troops from and give up the island of Malta to France. It is fair to presume, therefore, from the studied design and great effort that England made for the conquest of Louisiana, that if the British flag had ever once floated over New Orleans it would never have been hauled down without a struggle. Under these circumstances, it is not arrogating too much praise to Captain Reid and his heroic crew to give them the credit of not only having struck the fatal blow that effected the hopeless ruin of the grand scheme of the British Ministry, but saved the United States Government from a terrible disaster, and the country from an incalculable calamity.

SKETCH OF THE LIFE OF CAPTAIN SAMUEL CHESTER REID.

There are but few men whose lives, in a career of over threescore and ten, have been more distinguished for the historical and romantic incidents which have attended them than that of Captain Samuel Chester Reid, the late heroic commander of the United States private-armed brig-of-war General Armstrong. The preceding pages have given the details of a battle that immortalized his name and called forth the admiration of the world.

Captain Reid was highly honored on his return to the United States. He arrived at Amelia Island in a Portuguese brig from Fayal with his officers and crew, on the fifteenth of November, 1814, and proceeded thence to St. Mary's, Fla. He received ovations all the way from Savannah to New York. At Richmond, Va., the members of the Legislature gave him a dinner, at which Gov. W. C. Nichols, Mr. Stevenson, Speaker of the House, Mr. William Wirt, and others were present. The legislature of his own State, New York, in April, 1815, passed resolutions of thanks to Captain Reid, his officers and crew "for their intrepid valor in thus gloriously maintaining the honor of the American flag," and voted him a gold sword. The owners of the General Armstrong and his fellow-citizens of New York City presented to Captain Reid an elegant service of silver plate, "as a mark of the high sense entertained for his distinguished skill and valor" in the defence of the Armstrong.

Captain Reid was not only known as the valorous commander of the Armstrong; he was equally conspicuous in devoting his talents and genius to the benefit and service of his country. He designed the present form of the United States flag as adopted by Congress in 1818, and which was first hoisted on the Capitol on the thirteenth of April of that year. In 1821, he invented and erected the first marine telegraph between the Highlands of the Neversink on Staten Island, and the Battery at New York City. He also designed and published a national code of signals for all vessels belonging to the United States. He reorganized and perfected regulations for governing the pilots of the port of New York, and had the pilot boats numbered. Through his efforts and instigation he caused the Government to establish a lightship off Sandy Hook, the first ever constructed. In 1826 he invented a new system of land telegraphs, by means of which he satisfactorily demonstrated that a message could be sent from Washington city to New Orleans in two hours. A bill was before Congress for its adoption, when Morse's discovery superseded it. He likewise instituted and organized the Shipmasters' and Marine Society of New York, for the improvement of sea captains, and the support of their widows and children, and in many ways devoted himself to the cause of education, art, and science.

On the death of Captain Reid, twenty-eighth of January, 1861, the NEW YORK HERALD characterized the battle of the Armstrong as being "The Thermopylæ of the ocean," and in mentioning his services to his country, said:

"They are, aside from the romantic personal interest which hangs about them, among the most important events in the history of our nation. Reid was indeed a man of rare combinations, possessing great genius and talent, the courage of a lion, the adventurous spirit of a crusader, the taste of a poet, and the tenderness of a woman. He belonged to that old school of patriots of whom Paul Jones was the first and himself the last."

Captain Reid was born in the town of Norwich, State of Connecticut, on the twenty-fifth of August, 1783, the year of peace, just after the throes of the Revolution. He was the second and only surviving son of Lieutenant John Reid of the British navy, who was captured at New London, Conn., in October, 1778, while in command of a night-boat expedition sent out from the British squadron, under Admiral Hotham, which was then ravaging the coast. Lieutenant Reid was a son of Lord John Reid, of Glasgow, Scotland, and a lineal descendant of Henry Reid, Earl of Orkney, and Lord High Admiral to Robert III. (Bruce), King of Scotland, in 1393. His great-grandson was William Reid, of Aikenhead, county of Clackmannan, whose son, Robert Reid, became Bishop of Orkney in 1543, and these were the progenitors of Lieutenant John Reid, the father of Capt. Samuel Chester Reid.

During the time Lieutenant Reid was a prisoner and held as hostage, he resigned his commission under George III., and espoused the American cause. In February, 1781, he married Miss Rebecca Chester, of Norwich, by whom he had but two sons, the eldest of which died young, leaving Samuel Chester Reid the only child. Miss Chester was a descendant of the fourth generation of Captain Samuel Chester, formerly an officer of the British navy, who, in 1662, emigrated to Connecticut and settled in New London. He was a son of Sir Robert Chester, who was knighted by James I., in 1603, and was a direct descendant of the Earls of Chester, through whom he was collaterally connected with Robert I. (Bruce), King of Scotland. John, the son of Captain Samuel Chester, was the great-grandfather of Rebecca, and in 1685 was one of the magistrates of the upper house of the assembly of the colony of Connecticut. His son, the second John Chester,

CEREMONIES OF THE PRESENTATION OF "LONG TOM," BY PORTUGAL, TO THE UNITED STATES, 1886.

succeeded his father as magistrate in 1747, and who was the grandfather of Miss Chester. His son, the third John Chester, served at Bunker Hill and the Battle of Lexington in 1775, and was a colonel in Brigadier-General Wadsworth's Connecticut brigade. He was a delegate to the Connecticut Convention in January, 1788, which ratified the Constitution of the United States. He was the father of Rebecca Chester, who was the mother of Captain Samuel Chester Reid.

Captain Reid, following the inherited vocation of his forefathers, went to sea from New York, at the early age of eleven, on a voyage to the West Indies. He was captured by a French privateer, and carried into Basseterre, Guadeloupe, where he was confined for six months. He subsequently served as acting midshipman on the sloop-of-war Baltimore with Commodore Thomas Truxton, who commanded the West India squadron. He commanded the brig Merchant, of New York, when only twenty years of age.

Captain Reid married, at New York City, on the eighth of June, 1813, Mary, daughter of Captain Nathan Jennings, of Willington, Conn., who volunteered as private at the Battle of Lexington, April, 1775. He afterwards enlisted and served in Captain Willes's fifth company of General Spencer's brigade. He crossed the Delaware with General Washington, and commanded a company at the Battle of Trenton, twenty-sixth of December, 1776, being distinguished for gallant services on the field.

HISTORY OF THE GUN "LONG TOM" OF THE UNITED STATES PRIVATE-ARMED BRIG-OF-WAR GENERAL ARMSTRONG.

The following extraordinary and romantic history of this gun was furnished by Commander A. S. Crowninshield, of the United States Navy.

In the month of October, 1798, the French line of battle-ship Hoche, of eighty-four guns, was captured by a British squadron, commanded by Sir John B. Warren (afterwards well known on our coast), and sent into an English port where her armament was offered for sale. Colonel Ephraim Bowen, of Providence, and Mr. John B. Murray, of New York, who were in England at the time, purchased her main battery of forty-two pounder cannons on speculation, and shipped them to New York.

There they were sold to the United States Government, to be mounted in the harbor, and General Ebenezer Stevens was appointed to inspect them. He rejected one gun, in consequence of a severe indentation on the muzzle, that somewhat affected the bore, which, however, was afterwards reamed out by the owners, and the gun was retained by them.

In 1804, Mr. Murray, in conjunction with others, entered into a contract with the Emperor of Hayti for a supply of munitions of war, to carry on his conflict with France. These gentlemen fitted out three vessels, all of which were armed for the protection of that island against the French. Among them was the "Samson," Captain Palmer, a large ship carrying fourteen guns, with this rejected forty-two-pounder mounted amidships on a pivot.

Its first service was the carrying away of a foremast of a large French privateer, which gave chase to the little squadron, and thus disabled her from further pursuit. The contract with Hayti having been completed and the little fleet disposed of, Mr. Murray purchased the Samson, which vessel he forthwith disarmed for the merchant service.

This was in 1807, when the "big gun" being dismounted was laid on the bulkhead in South Street, New York City, where it remained for several years in that situation, when it was finally transferred to the foundry of Robert McQueen in Duane Street, in view of being recast in old metal. While there, the War of 1812 was declared, and New York was alive with preparations for fitting out privateers. Among them was the celebrated brig General Armstrong, commanded by Captain Samuel Chester Reid, which vessel was built by Adam and Noah Brown, the eminent shipbuilders, who purchased the "big gun" at the price of two hundred and fifty dollars.

It was mounted on a pivot amidships, and remained there through her cruises until she was finally blockaded in the bay of Fayal, one of the Azore islands belonging to Portugal, in September, 1814, by a large British squadron, whose commander, in violation of the laws of neutrality and all rules of war, attempted her capture. The gun, Long Tom, was brought to bear with terrible execution against this powerful squadron, resulting in their defeat and a loss of over three hundred of their officers and men. The superior forces of the British squadron finally prevailed, so far as to cause the destruction of the Armstrong, which after being scuttled on the beach and abandoned by her crew, the British set her on fire, when she became a total wreck.

Long Tom was afterwards fished up from its watery grave, and was mounted in the Castle of Santa Cruz, at Fayal, where it had been exhibited as a relic of this wonderful battle for the past seventy-eight years, before it was transhipped back again to New York. It is a singular coincidence that this gun should have remained at Fayal just the period of Captain Reid's life, who died at the age of seventy-eight.

The return of the gun to the United States was effected through the means of Colonel Sam C. Reid, the son of the commander of the Armstrong, who visited Fayal in 1890, with a view of obtaining a sketch of the battle ground and the harbor and bay, for his work on the Memoirs of his father. He was conducted to the Castle of Santa Cruz by

Mr. Samuel W. Dabney, then the United States consul at Fayal, and was introduced to Long Tom, which had caused so much fame and celebrity.

In September, 1891, Colonel Reid addressed a letter to President Harrison requesting our minister at Lisbon, General Geo. S. Batcheller, be instructed to make an amicable demand for the transfer of this gun to our Government. To this request the King of Portugal, Don Carlos I., most graciously consented, and the transfer of the gun to the American Minister was made at Fayal on the twelfth of May, 1892, with great ceremony by a commission of the Portuguese military officers, and in the presence of the troops of the garrison.

The following is a translated copy of the official report deposited in the Portuguese military archives at Lisbon:

Headquarters of the Military Commander
of the Western Azores, Horta,

Twelfth of May, 1892.

Record of the delivery of the forty-two-pounder, Long Tom, now being in the Castle of Santa Cruz, described by the letters, F. L. S. P. 17 C, to his Excellency, Mr. Batcheller, Minister of the United States of North America, in Portugal.

On the twelfth day of the month of May, 1892, at twelve o'clock in the day, there assembled at the Secretariate of the Military Commander of the Western Azores, a commission composed of the following officers: Francisco Alfonso da Costa Chaves e Mello, Captain of the Eleventh Regiment of Chasseurs; Bernardo Pereira de Vasconcellos, First Lieutenant of the Second Company of the Garrison Artillerymen; and José Ignacio da Silva, ensign in the Eleventh Regiment of Chasseurs, to proceed to deliver the forty-two-pounder, Long Tom, to his Excellency, Mr. Batcheller, Minister of the

United States of North America, in Portugal, who is present at this Secretariate.

His Excellency having expressed a desire that the delivery should be made immediately, the Commission proceeded to the Castle of Santa Cruz, in this town of Horta, and there in the presence of their Excellencies, José Estanislau Ventura, Lieutenant Colonel of Infantry, and Military Commander of the Western Azores; Lewis Dexter, Consul of the United States of America, in this Island; Francisco da Nazareth Vieira, Lieutenant and Sheriff; and Alfredo de Sampaio Leite, Ensign in the Eleventh Regiment of Chasseurs, was recognized the gun F. L. S. P. 17 C. by his Excellency the Minister referred to, as being the forty-two-pounder, "Long Tom," wherefore it was delivered to him, and at the same time this record was drawn up which is signed by his Excellency Mr. Batcheller, and by the members of the Commission:

GEORGE S. BATCHELLER,
Minister of the United States of America.

FRANCISCO ALFONSO DA COSTA CHAVES E MELLO,
Captain of the Eleventh Regiment of Chasseurs.

BERNADO PEREIRO DE VASCONCELLOS,
First Lieutenant of the Second Company of Artillerymen of the Garrison.

JOSE IGNACIO DE SILVA,
Ensign of the Eleventh Regiment of Chasseurs.

Executed in due form. Headquarters of Military Commander of the Western Azores, Horta, twelfth of May, 1892.

JOSE ESTANISLAU VENTURA,
Lieutenant Colonel of Infantry.

It is but justice to say that great credit is due to General Batcheller for his patriotic zeal and diplomatic energy in obtaining the consent of the Portuguese Government to deliver up Long Tom. It was the intention of the Secretary of the Navy, Hon. B. F. Tracy, to send a ship-of-war to Fayal for the gun, but as no vessel was available at the time, Messrs. Bensaude & Co., the enterprising owners of the Insular Navigation Steamship Company, of Lisbon, which runs monthly from Lisbon *via* the Azores to New York, generously offered to bring it over free of charge, which offer was accepted by our Government. The gun was shipped from Fayal on the eighth of April, on the splendid steamship "Vega," Captain Da Rossa, which arrived at New York on the night of the eighteenth of April, 1893.

The return of this famous gun to America, after its seclusion of over three quarters of a century in the ancient Castle of Santa Cruz, has revived the historic glory of its brilliant exploits, and created the greatest public interest.

At the request of that gallant, patriotic naval officer, Commodore Richard W. Meade, whose genius and enterprise designed the celebrated model battleship Illinois, at Chicago, this gun, on its arrival at New York, was sent to the Exposition as one of the naval exhibits, together with the portrait and battle sabre of Captain Reid.

THE FLAG OF THE UNITED STATES. — ITS ORIGIN AND HISTORY. ITS PRESENT FORM DESIGNED BY CAPTAIN SAMUEL CHESTER REID.

It is important that every American citizen should become familiar with the history of the flag of his country. The following account is from the most authentic historical records:

The American flag in 1775 was "the British union with the crosses of St. George and St. Andrew in a red field," and was displayed at New York on a liberty pole with the inscription, "George Rex and the Liberties of America." It is a little singular that the first flag adopted as our national ensign by our ships of war consisted of horizontal stripes with the British union still retained in a canton, but was afterwards replaced by the stars on a blue field.

There is no question of the fact that the origin of our national flag was taken from the coat of arms of the Washington family, which was constituted of stars and bars. In 1776 the construction of the first national standard with the stars and stripes took place in Philadelphia under the personal direction of General Washington and a committee of the old Continental Congress. The first flags bore twelve stars in a circle, as then only twelve States had ratified the Articles of Confederation. On June 14, 1777, Congress resolved that "the flag of the United States" be thirteen stripes, alternate white and red, and the union be thirteen white stars in a blue field.

On January 13, 1794, after two new States had been admitted, Congress passed an act that the stripes and stars be increased to fifteen each. Upon the admission of new States subsequently stripes and stars were being added to the flag, which soon rendered it unwieldy and destroyed its form and perspicuity.

On the admission of the State of Indiana into the Union, in 1816, a resolution was introduced at the second session of the Fourteenth Congress in the House, by Mr. Wendover, of New York, to inquire into the expediency of altering "the flag of the United States." Afterwards the Committee on Naval Affairs called on Captain Samuel Chester Reid, of New York, who was in Washington at the time, late commander of the brig-of-war General Armstrong, to make a permanent design for the flag. He reduced the stripes to thirteen, to represent the original States, and to add a star to the union for each new State.

. He presented two forms of the flag, one with the stars formed into one great star in the union expressing significantly the symbol, "E Pluribus Unum," for our ships and steamers in the merchant service, and the other with the stars in parallel lines for the halls of Congress, our ships of war, and public buildings. Congress approved of the design by "an act to establish the flag of the United States," passed thirty-first of March, 1818, Fifteenth Congress, first session, and approved by President Monroe on April 4, 1818.

The first flag of the present design was made by the wife of Captain Reid, assisted by some young ladies, at her house in New York City, on Cherry Street, near Franklin Square, and was first hoisted on the Capitol on the thirteenth of April, 1818, seventy-five years ago.

The lines of Drake are here appropriate:

> "Flag of the free heart's only home,
>   By angel hands to valor given;
> Thy stars have lit the welkin dome,
>   And all thy hues were born in heaven."

The genius that designed the settled form and permanency of the United States flag was most aptly chosen. No braver or more gallant sailor could have been selected for the task — none more deserving than he, who had won the world's applause and immortal fame at the battle of Fayal with a British squadron in 1814.

A brilliant September midnight moon lit up with its silvery sheen the waters of the bay and the walls of Horta, burnishing the towering volcanic peak of Mount Pico, which seemed excited to eruption as it looked down upon the battle scene below. The American ensign floated defiantly from the peak of the General Armstrong, amid the roar and smoke of guns and the clash of steel — then the battle cry and shout of victory rang out upon the air, and re-echoed again and again over the bay and the hills of Horta. The stars in that flag that night were silvered with a brilliant lustre, which not even the moonbeams dancing on the waves of the bay, blood-red with the human gore of England's bravest and best, could make more dazzling than the splendors of that victory!

It would seem that Drake was painting this scene, when he wrote:

> "Flag of the seas! on ocean's wave
> Thy stars shall glitter o'er the brave,
> When death careering on the gale
> Sweeps darkly round the swelling sail,
> And frighted waves rush wildly back
> Before the broadside's reeling rack,
> The dying wanderer on the sea
> Shall look at once to heaven and thee —
> And smile, to see thy splendors fly,
> In triumph, o'er his closing eye."

The prowess of nations and the heroism on their battle-fields have been inspired and achieved by the emblems of their battle-banners and flags, stimulating their warriors to deeds of valor and the highest courage. Carlyle says: "We see in flags the divine idea of duty, of heroic daring, and sometimes of freedom and right."

THE FLAG THAT REID DESIGNED.

> This is the flag that Reid designed;
> Whose splendors by his art enshrined,
> Transformed anew the stripes and stars
> That proudly triumphed in our wars.
> Long as it waves 'twill bear his name,
> And tell of his immortal fame.

Who was the hero of Fayal?
A battle that exceeded all
 E'er fought upon the seas,
A British squadron, ten to one,
He vanquished with his "Long Tom" gun,
 And brought proud Albion to her knees.

'Twas Reid, who on that fearful night
Wielded his sword with giant's might;
'Twas Reid, amid the cannon's roar,
When steel flashed steel reeking with gore,
In British blood he bathed anew
The crimson in his flag so true.

He added lustre still more bright,
By this heroic, gallant fight,
And to his country glory gave,
Not knowing that he was to save
The victory which Jackson won,
Revenging the fall of Washington!

S. C. REID.

ADMIRAL SIR THOMAS LORD COCHRANE AND CAPTAIN SAMUEL CHESTER REID.

The London correspondent of the Baltimore Sun, in April, 1879, gave the following interesting statement in relation to the unjust treatment of the British naval hero, Admiral Sir Thomas Cochrane, by his government, whose name is historically connected with an American naval hero of equal, if not of greater renown, Captain Samuel Chester Reid:

"You, good reader from 'north of the Tweed,' may call to memory the name of Thomas Lord Cochrane; and you who know better the banks of the Potomac may not be unmindful of this naval name. Last week this name was given justice in the election of a Scotch peer, and that peer was of the loins of Lord Cochrane, the late Earl of Dundonald. In European waters, on the Atlantic and Pacific oceans, the name of Lord Dundonald is a household word with readers of naval history. A vicious sentence of years hung over him, and an enormous fine paid by the subscriptions of two million six hundred and forty thousand persons at one penny each, told him of his persecution and popularity at one and the same time. He was expelled from the House of Commons, but at once re-elected by the people of Westminster. By piecemeal his rights were restored in part when the sun of his life was setting. On a twilight eve in 1860 he died, bequeathing his claim against the British Government to his grandson, Douglas, the present Lord Cochrane. Last year all the back pay and rights of the great naval hero were fully paid and handed over to this Lord Cochrane, and on Tuesday last the son of the ill-treated hero was elected a peer of Scotland, and his son, the aforesaid Lord Cochrane, beheld the memory and name of his grandfather and his father thus slowly but surely reinstated in the roll of history. How many men in America have been similarly ill-treated, but not similarly justified and rewarded!"

There is a remarkable incident connecting the names of these two naval heroes with each other, and though as distant as the first and last links of a chain, they are nevertheless closely associated in both English and American history, the one having exercised a fatal destiny over the other.

As we have seen, but for Captain Reid's heroic defence of the Armstrong in defeating and delaying Lloyd's Squadron, Admiral Sir Thomas Cochrane, Earl of Dundonald, might have been a victorious hero, with his fleet triumphantly anchored in the Mississippi, off New Orleans, and the British flag of the Cross of St. George proclaiming the conquest of an American India!

Thus Captain Reid's fame and name are singularly linked with that of Sir Admiral Cochrane's, the late Earl of Dundonald, who died in 1860, and the former in 1861, without the reward of justice by either of their governments.

THE GENERAL ARMSTRONG.— A NEW SONG.

TUNE.—" VIVE-LA."

The following song was composed by the general officers of the Armstrong on their voyage from Fayal to the United States. It is in the old ballad style of that day, and is worthy of preservation.

> Come, listen to a gallant action,
>   Which was fought in Fayal Bay,
> By the saucy General Armstrong;
>   From eight P. M. till break of day.

Chorus.—Hail! the saucy General Armstrong:
  Reid's immortalized her name —
Her cannon dealt death and destruction
  To furbish young Columbia's fame.

> Plantagenet, Rota, and Carnation
>   Thought with her to have rare sport,
> Sent in their boats, with an intention
>   To cut her out of a neutral port.—*Chorus.*

> At eight, four boats commenc'd the action,
>   Which fifteen minutes' work laid low;
> Quarters next came in rotation,
>   Which on them we did bestow.—*Chorus.*

Fourteen boats, with men five hundred,
    At midnight made the grand attack;
In forty minutes half their number
    Were killed and wounded, falling back.—*Chorus.*

Britain's killed in both engagements,
    Amounted to three hundred men;
Fifty more of them were wounded—
    The rest retreated back again.—*Chorus.*

The number killed on board the General,
    It doth grieve us to relate,
The falling of Lieutenant Williams,
    And one man we do regret.—*Chorus.*

Two lieutenants more were wounded,
    And likewise five of our men;
But we've got them safely landed,
    And recovering fast again.—*Chorus.*

Then at break of day next morning,
    The sloop of war got under way,
And opened her broadside upon us,
    British courage to display.—*Chorus.*

Lest she should fall in their possession,
    We thought it prudent her to sink;
Which was put in execution,
    And thus the General became extinct.—*Chorus.*

Then by the British she was boarded
    (Who finding her partly destroyed
Set her on fire) when thus abandoned,
    By command of Captain Lloyd.—*Chorus.*

> Although we could not save the General,
> Columbia's fame we held in view;
> We have chastis'd the haughty Britons
> With our little Yankee crew.—*Chorus.*

THE CELEBRATED CASE OF THE BRIG GENERAL ARMSTRONG.

The final destruction of the brig General Armstrong by the British squadron in the neutral waters of the island of Fayal, belonging to Portugal, in violation of the laws of neutrality, became a subject of earnest diplomatic correspondence between this government and Portugal for over forty years from the time of its occurrence.

The Portuguese government had at once acknowledged its liability to this government, and made a peremptory demand on Great Britain for satisfaction and indemnification for the violation of the neutrality of its territory and the destruction of the Armstrong. The British government made an apology to Portugal for the violation of their neutrality, and indemnity for the loss of property sustained by the firing of the British warships, but refused to pay for the burning of the Armstrong, for which Portugal was responsible to the United States for not having, as a neutral power, protected the Armstrong.

The British government contended that the American brig *first* fired into the British boats, which were merely reconnoitering, without any cause or provocation!

After years of fruitless efforts to obtain any satisfaction from Portugal, that government, in 1843, wholly denied its liability, and boldly declared that the Americans had first violated the neutrality of their port!

This government, under Van Buren's administration, then abandoned the claim, on the ground that "argument and importunity had been exhausted, and the circumstances did not warrant it in having recourse to any other weapons."

Mr. Sam C. Reid, Jr., who was then prosecuting this claim in behalf of his father, and the owners, officers, and crew of the brig, procured its revival in 1845, under Mr. Polk's administration.

It may be interesting to the reader to give the following coincidence in relation to this claim. During the war with Mexico Mr. Reid was attached to Captain Ben McCulloch's scouting company of the celebrated Jack Hays' regiment of Texas Rangers. In August, 1846, the army of General Taylor was on its march from Comargo to Monterey. Mr. Reid had been sent with a despatch from the front to General Taylor, and after some friendly conversation, in taking his leave, Mr. Reid remarked, "Well, General, we may never meet again, but I think I know the popular pulse of our people well enough to predict that, if you win the battle of Monterey, you will become President of the United States!" The General laughed, and expressing his incredulity, said, as Mr. Reid was mounting his horse, "Reid, when I get to be President your father shall have his claim against Portugal." "Good," replied Reid, "I'll hold you to it."

General Taylor became President, and kept his word. He instructed Mr. John M. Clayton, Secretary of State in 1849, to renew this claim against Portugal. That government, backed up by England, refused to pay the claim, but urged that it be submitted to a third power for arbitration. Mr. Clayton declined to arbitrate so just a claim, and pledged the national honor never to consent to submit to so humiliating a proposition.

Mr. Jas. B. Clay, our minister at Lisbon, son of Henry Clay, was then instructed to make a peremptory demand on Portugal, and our Mediterranean squadron proceeded, in July, 1850, up the river Tagus to Lisbon to receive the *ultimatum*.

Portugal positively declined, and Mr. Clay took his passports and left for the United States. The case was being prepared to submit to Congress when General Taylor died, on the ninth of July, 1850.

Mr. Fillmore's administration succeeded. The proposition to arbitrate was renewed, and accepted by this government in September, 1850, notwithstanding the national faith was plighted never to consent to tarnish its spotless escutcheon. Louis Napoleon, *President* of the French republic, was chosen arbiter, under a treaty which excluded the important testimony of the claimants. In 1853, when Louis Napoleon had become *Emperor*, he decided the case in favor of Portugal and England, in violation of the treaty.

In 1854, an appeal was made to Congress; unanimous reports were made in favor of the claim; it passed the Senate twice, and was lost in the House the last time for the want of two of a quorum! In the debate in the Senate, in January, 1855, Senator James A. Bayard, in referring to Louis Napoleon's decision, said:

"Well, sir, looking on that decision as an atrocity throughout, unsustainable by any known principle of law, but a perversion of facts from beginning to end, I cannot believe that it would have been made if our government had not rejected the right of the claimant to be heard by his counsel, or by its own agents, before the authority deputed by the French Emperor to examine the case. I therefore conceive that this party has lost a decision in this case from what I term the gross neglect of our government, arising from a misconstruction of a treaty which does not preclude the right to be heard. . . . In this country no man who wishes to be heard in defence of his rights should be refused a fair opportunity to be heard in vindication of those rights when they are to be decided upon. It is on this ground that I shall vote in favor of the claim as an obligation on the government."

The case was finally referred to the Court of Claims, which first decided in favor of the claimants, then, on a rehearing, it reversed its decision, but admitted the equity of the case. It was again submitted to Congress in 1858; unanimous reports were made in its favor, but, as usual, it failed for want of action.

Twenty years had elapsed. All the original claimants had died. They had sunk into unrequited graves, with the ingratitude of a government oblivious to their heroism and the great benefits they had rendered to their country, for their only requiem.

Their claims on the government had become forgotten in the dark labyrinths of the past, and the waves of time had washed over them as a long-abandoned wreck.

During the forty-fifth Congress, Mr. Reid under these hopeless circumstances, renewed this claim for the benefit of the heirs. At the session of the forty-sixth Congress, unanimous reports were made in favor of the bill, which had passed the Senate and lay on the speaker's table. On the last day of the session, Hon. Proctor Knott, of Kentucky, stood on the floor of the House from noon until midnight in vain endeavoring to get the recognition of the Speaker, and the bill, with its usual fatality, again failed to pass.

At the first session of the forty-seventh Congress, 1882, unanimous reports were again made in favor of the bill. The Honorable W. W. Rice, of Massachusetts, that able and distinguished jurist and statesman, from the Committee on Foreign Affairs of the House, in his report said:

"Senate committees and House committees have many times reported in its favor, and never against it, and yet it is an unquestionable fact that the owners of the privateer General Armstrong, burnt by a British squadron in the neutral waters of Fayal, in September, 1814, after a defence by her crew which won the admiration of the world and the gratitude of their country, have never been paid for the property they then lost, and their representatives now stand where their fathers stood, at the doors of Congress, still waiting for tardy justice."

At the same session, the late Hon. George H. Pendleton, of Ohio, in his masterly and exhaustive report from the Committee on Foreign relations of the Senate, thus alludes to this claim:

"The event out of which the claim arose is most creditable to the valor and skill of American seamen, and in its remoter influences evidently secured victory to the American arms at New Orleans. The accompanying papers will give the narrative, which, in romantic incidents, almost equals a tale of the imagination."

The bill for the relief of the captain, owners, officers and crew of the brig General Armstrong finally passed at this session, April, 1882, appropriating the sum of seventy thousand seven hundred and thirty-nine dollars, which simply was for the actual loss of the owners for the brig, and for the personal loss of the effects of the officers and crew, without interest for sixty-eight years, the period for which the claimants had been awaiting the long delayed justice of this government, and which had been demanded from the government of Portugal.

It is a remarkable and astonishing fact, that through the blunders of the Department of State in illegally distributing this appropriation, a claim is still pending, unadjusted at this late day, for a portion of the sum thus awarded.

This case occupied the attention of all Europe at the time of the unjust award of Louis Napoleon, which was afterward denounced by the Baron de Cussy, of France, in his great work on "International Law and the Rights of Neutrals," in which this case is cited as the most remarkable of the *causes celebre*.

The Armstrong Claim has been given a world-wide celebrity and notoriety, by its having been dramatized and made the foundation for the comedy of "The Senator," written by David D. Lloyd and Sidney Rosenfeld, and in which Mr. Wm. H. Crane has achieved such distinguished laurels.

If the Press of the United States will, in their generosity and patriotism, advocate the raising of this monument to Captain Reid, by the contributions of THE PEOPLE in the purchase of this pamphlet to effect the same, there is no question of its success.

THE FIGHT OF THE "ARMSTRONG" PRIVATEER.

BY JAMES JEFFREY ROCHE.

(From the *Century Magazine*, June, 1892.)

Tell the story to your sons
    Of the gallant days of yore,
When the brig of seven guns
    Fought the fleet of seven score.
From the set of sun till morn, through the long September
    night —
Ninety men against two thousand, and the ninety won the
    fight —
    In the harbor of Fayal the Azore.

Three lofty British ships came a-sailing to Fayal;
One was a line-of-battle ship, and two were frigates tall;
Nelson's valiant men of war, brave as Britons ever are,
Manned the guns they served so well at Aboukir and Trafalgar.
Lord Dundonald and his fleet at Jamaica, far away,
Waited eager for their coming, fretted sore at their delay.
There was work for men of mettle, ere the shameful peace
    was made,

And the sword was overbalanced in the sordid scales of
        trade :
There were rebel knaves to swing, there were prisoners to
        bring
Home in fetters to old England for the glory of the King!

At the setting of the sun and the ebbing of the tide
Came the great ships, one by one, with their portals opened
        wide,
And their cannon frowning down on the castle and the town
And the privateer that lay close inside :
Came the eighteen-gun Carnation and the Rota, forty-four,
And the triple-decked Plantagenet an admiral's pennon bore ;
And the privateer grew smaller as their topmasts towered
        taller,
And she bent her springs and anchored by the castle on the
        shore.

Spake the noble Portuguese to the stranger: " Have no fear;
They are neutral waters, these, and your ship is sacred here
As if fifty stout armadas stood to shelter you from harm.
For the honor of the Briton will defend you from his arm."
But the privateersman said, " Well we know the Englishmen,
And their faith is written red in the Dartmoor slaughter-pen.
Come what fortune God may send, we will fight them to the
        end,
And the mercy of the sharks may spare us then."

"Seize the pirate where she lies!" cried the English admiral :
" If the Portuguese protect her, all the worse for Portugal!"
And four launches at his bidding leaped impatient for the fray.
Speeding shoreward where the Armstrong grim and dark and
        ready lay.
Twice she hailed and gave them warning; but the feeble
        menace scorning,

On they came in splendid silence till a cable's length away—
Then the Yankee pivot spoke; Pico's thousand echoes woke,
And four baffled, beaten launches drifted helpless on the bay.

Then the wrath of Lloyd arose till the lion roared again,
And he called out all his launches, and he called five hundred men;
And he gave the word, "No quarter!" and he sent them forth to smite.
Heaven help the foe before him when the Briton comes in might!
Heaven helped the little Armstrong in her hour of bitter need;
God Almighty nerved the heart and guided well the arm of Reid.

Launches to port and starboard, launches forward and aft,
Fourteen launches all together striking the little craft.
They hacked at the boarding nettings, they swarmed above the rail;
But the Long Tom roared from his pivot and the grape-shot fell like hail;
Pike and pistol and cutlass, and hearts that knew not fear,
Bulwarks of brawn and mettle, guarded the privateer.
And ever where fight was fiercest the form of Reid was seen;
Ever where foes drew nearest, his quick sword fell between.
  Once in the deadly strife
   The boarders' leader pressed
   Forward of all the rest,
  Challenging life for life;
   But ere their blades had crossed,
   A dying sailor tossed
   His pistol to Reid, and cried,
  "Now riddle the lubber's hide!"
But the privateersman laughed and flung the weapon aside,

And he drove his blade to the hilt, and the foeman gasped
    and died.
Then the boarders took to their launches, laden with hurt
    and dead,
But little with glory burdened, and out of the battle fled.

Now the tide was at flood again, and the night was almost
    done.
When the sloop-of-war came up with her odds of two to one,
And she opened fire: but the Armstrong answered her, gun
    for gun,
And the gay Carnation wilted in half an hour of sun.

Then the Armstrong, looking seaward, saw the mighty seventy-four,
With her triple tier of cannon, drawing slowly to the shore.
And the dauntless captain said: "Take our wounded and
    our dead,
Bear them tenderly to land, for the Armstrong's days are
    o'er:
But no foe shall tread her deck, and no flag above it wave—
To the ship that saved our honor we will give a shipman's
    grave."
So they did as he commanded, and they bore their mates to
    land,
With the figurehead of Armstrong and the good sword in
    his hand.
Then they turned the Long Tom downward, and they
    pierced her oaken side,
And they cheered her, and they blessed her, and they sunk
    her in the tide.

      Tell the story to your sons,
        When the haughty stranger boasts

Of his mighty ships and guns
And the muster of his hosts.
How the word of God was witnessed in the gallant days of
yore.
When the twenty fled from one ere the rising of the sun.
In the harbor of Fayal the Azore.

www.ingramcontent.com/pod-product-compliance
Lightning Source LLC
Chambersburg PA
CBHW020252090426
42735CB00010B/1897